Takeaway
Georgie Woodhead

NEWPOETSLIST

the poetry business

Published 2021 by
New Poets List
The Poetry Business
Campo House,
54 Campo Lane,
Sheffield S1 2EG

Copyright © Georgie Woodhead 2021
All Rights Reserved

ISBN 978-1-912196-62-3
eBook ISBN 978-1-912196-63-0
Typeset by The Poetry Business
Printed by Biddles, Sheffield

Smith|Doorstop Books are a member of Inpress:
www.inpressbooks.co.uk

Distributed by NBN International, 1 Deltic Avenue,
Rooksley, Milton Keynes MK13 8LD

The Poetry Business gratefully acknowledges
the support of Arts Council England.

Contents

5	Takeaway
6	When my uncle stood at the top of the office block roof
7	Backtrack
8	Women who stand on one leg
9	Baby
11	Tim
13	Collins
14	Monkey Men
15	The Boxer
17	Pebbles
18	Why Mum Bit Her Tongue at the Crematorium
19	Baba's Burgers
20	What I Know About Alice
22	Candyfloss
23	Poltergeist
24	Dumplings

Takeaway

After Sammy Gooch

After the explosion, we got a Chinese takeaway and sat
pulled up outside Asda crunching through prawn crackers
that looked like freeze-dried jellyfish. Our mouths too busy

to speak about the bodies we saw rag-doll flung
before the sound even cracked. The apartment windows
shattering in unison like a magic trick. The way water

and air were sucked out so the world became a dust-flood
that crept under our tongues and hid like ants. Steam choked
the car windscreen like a sauna and we glugged our Coke,

tangy and cold, while I replayed, in slow-mo, the man
who hobbled out onto the street dragging a snapped
toothpick leg. The girl with a dark red brisket gash

across her cheek like raw steak with tarmac-black
grains peppercorning her skin. Instead of words,
we kept eating, and you turned on the radio to hits

from the '80s, and we dipped into the sweetness
of hoisin sauce, trying not to think of its sticky darkness,
our lips moving along to Jimmy – *Don't Leave Me This Way*.

When my uncle stood at the top of the office block roof

he swayed from side to side, half-glugged bottle locked
in his burning fingers, his silhouette framed by the black hole of night,
flecks of scornful planets blinked behind his back. The whole world
stretched out in front of him like the sides of a fallen down box,
and his eyes had been opened, and stared open as his shoulders
shook. His feet stumbled back and forth towards the edge,
the leather of his shoes creaking in protest against the gutter.

When the bar had closed and we were tossed out, left to stroll
with our hands shoved in our pockets like tree stumps rooted in earth,
we heard his bottle, a free-fall smash into green teeth on paving slabs.
He leaned over his small carnage in the same silence as we did,
our mouths open, eyelids pinned apart, necks turned like twisted cloth.
And him, with his frown slashed thin, disappointed, eyebrows folded
as if he had honestly expected anything different.

Backtrack

I was born in a house where everything happens
backwards. My sister sits cross-legged on her rocket ship
duvet cover, sucks salty water back into her eyes.

The mattress pushes her off. The shape of thick thighs,
legs in black tights, bent like cupid's bows, un-press from the bed.
She stands over the broken bits of lamp lying shattered

like a skeleton on the blue rug. It lifts itself back to the table,
and the kiss of the lightbulb seals a red-grinning blister
to her palm. She un-cups its new-born head, leaves it glowing

and un-scorched next to her jigsaw and walks backwards
out the room. Downstairs my father heals my mother's wounds
by pulling bruises from her eyes with his fist. She snorts

a little dribble of blood back through her nostrils as if it's nothing,
like charming a snake back into the basket. Then she lassoes words
with her red-chilli tongue, swallows them whole into her throat.

I can see how they slip down the inside of her neck and how much
she regrets everything, in the house where we all spit food
back onto our plates because we don't want to taste

the static stuck to our words. When we talk, it's in-between
regurgitating chickpeas speared like love-struck hearts at the end
of forks. On the TV *I'm playful* sounds like *Love, help me.*

Women who stand on one leg

have half a smile they unwrap
on special occasions, such as birthdays.
The bones in their face are high set and stiff
like scaffolding. They unravel conversation
from their tongues like dough from a rolling pin.

Women who stand on one leg have difficulty
moving around. They prefer to pose
in front of mirrors, practicing their jelly hips,
creaming their marzipan skin,
polishing their peppermint teeth.

At night, they sit on their beds and drop
rat poison into their eyes for the squealing
in their brains. The next day, they push
shopping trolleys around tiled floors
and fill them with desperate notes.

Women who stand on one leg swim
into the kitchen using their arms. They scoop
pig jelly from their beating meat hearts,
serve it for dinner, suck the sauce off
their fingers like ice lollies, and try

to fold their stomachs up
into tiny paper springs while carving
love letters into their hands.
They tell their husbands
not to chew so loud.

Baby

My mother presses her finger into her
swollen belly button, like she is trying to find
an eject switch, a shiny, puckered undo.

My father says she is beautiful the way she is
beach ball and water balloon. She feels
the hot blood stirring in her belly.

My father blows ripe raspberries onto
my mother and kisses the body under her skin,
presses his lips to the pink maggot

of its small mouth. He dreams of legs
swimming in her tummy, uncalloused
feet like white beach stones.

She sits on the toilet and cries,
tracksuit bottoms around her ankles.
She sees her pale, squashed legs

and says *fat*, and the word fills her mouth
like an olive. There are purple spider veins
running under her flesh. She pinches

the meat of her thighs with her nails,
leaves puncture marks, cradles the bulge
she wants to unpeel like an onion.

My father is excited by the whole thing,
buys a spinning mobile of crescent moons,
holds it up and turns the silver shapes

that look like toothy, halfway smiles. My mother
is the one carrying a tangle of limbs. She doesn't like
the idea of my tiny hands reaching out inside her.

Tim

His fingertips were pinched sandpaper.
I know this because he would squat down
and grab my chin
          and tell me how big
I was getting. Tim wore jeans with chains
hanging from them. He was not afraid
to kiss Mum
          in the kitchen. When she was washing
up he would run his hands over her arse
and bite her neck
          like nibbling a steak
before deciding it was good enough
to eat. Mum would giggle with a high-pitched sound
I had never heard before, her slim fingers
hugged by sticky
          yellow rubber gloves,
spotted with the insect eggs of white soap.
Tim dyed the tips of his hair blonde,
frosted like sugary cereal. He believed
that chewing
          a toothpick meant he didn't have to clean
his teeth. One time when I was dressed up for a wedding
he called me pretty
          and winked at me.
He took over the Playstation to play
Call of Duty on the
          burst blue beanbag,
spilling its insides out like a squashed slug.
He made machine gun noises with his teeth
and swallowed the room with his exhaust pipe

grease smell.
              He moved his CDs
onto the second shelf in the living room.
He microwaved ready-meal macaroni cheese –
stabbed the blistered plastic packaging
with a fork and hot air
                        spluttered out.
When mum was at work he left plates
stacked up in a tower of Pisa, brown sauce
smeared over them in muddy tyre marks.
He asked me about my day at school –
stood in my doorway
                  with his deodorant
of rusted metal. He says he is like a father
to me, sits on the side of my bed
and puts his hand
                  on my thigh.
He looks me in the eye and says,
                          'I mean it.'

Collins

Harry Collins was an artist who called himself a father.
He was bad jokes and foggy laughs, heavy breaths
that wheezed sometimes when words rolled in and out,
but never touched the air. He was things that he thought
better of saying. He was thick stubble and baggy jeans
like sacks, oversized white shirts, scuffed paper trainers.
He was toothpicks and dimples, rough skin and fidgeting,
a paintbrush dabbed on a brother's nose. He was a grin
that faded almost immediately, died on the lips, eyes
of china vases and blobs of wobbling ink. Harry Collins
was mixing colours and classical music, he was finding it hard
to get up and out of bed in the morning. He was yawning,
paint pallet in hand like a multi-coloured plastic hedgehog,
and canvases that were never quite right. He was sketches
when there were stones to skim. He was concentrating
when there was an orange hula-hoop struck in a tree,
and he was the opening lines of a story that stopped
when he shook his head like a bad dream.

Monkey Men

I peek round tall, paint-peeled doors
where the lights are dimmed, and there're men
who wear torches on their foreheads while they work,
car engines running in time with the radio.

Men with black fingerprints smudged across
their jaws that looks like stubble, spanners
hanging from racks on the wall, screwdrivers
in pencil pots. And they live in the clank and clunk

of metal slotting into place, they live with circuit wire
lines around their eyes, lying on their backs under warm
bodies of motors. Men who wipe their hands on dirty
cloths while they talk to customers, booming laughs

punching the air like crowbars. Men in oil-stained overalls,
drinking from flasks, who wipe their mouths on the backs
of hairy hands, watched by posters of women in bikinis
curling off the concrete walls. Men in workmen's gloves

and hitched-up belts, stood against car bonnets propped open,
smoke wheezing from the fuel caps like final breaths.
Men who point to the door, and tell me to *Fuck off*,
ears tinged red at the edges like thermometers.

Later, they'll sit, slouched in slacks, cards splayed
in greasy chip-fat fingers, and if I look through the hinges
of the garage door, I can just about see my own face
sooty, stretched out, staring back.

The Boxer

Before he gave it all up for pay monthly insurance, parents'
evenings, buy-to-let mortgages, sitting sighing in a suit and tie
at a desk above NatWest, an intercom attached to his ear,

he used to be a boxer, used to dance around the ring, fists held high
under the smoky lights, sweat balancing on his top lip, the crowd
roaring from the shadows, chanting his name. He used to live it,

the knockouts, the heavyweights, the shaven heads, the dripping
hunks of shoulder, arms tight and sinew-stretched like steak, muscles
twitching, sweat-soaked towels, the smell of tape being wrapped

round and round padded gloves. Now he spends his evenings
with his white socks propped up on the footrest, sipping cheap beer
watching Sky Sports over the curve of his belly. But some nights,

he lets his mind wander back into the ring, remembering the white towel
he wore like a scarf, the loudspeaker, the spotlights, the back pats
and shoulder slaps, the head roll click of bones in his neck,

and the musty, dim-lit back rooms with their overweight men,
stomachs bulging against belts like water balloons, cigars dangling
from sticky lips, counting notes, stacking coins. He remembers

the heat, the raw, wild energy of it all, beating his bare chest,
flakes of spit flying from his mouth. And then – face down,
blurry-eyed, blinking, black-bruised, referee counting him back

to fingers clicking on a keyboard, glasses scanning a screen,
the hiss of a can cracked open, ringing phones *How can I
help you?* being hung up on, hung over, hung out to dry.

And like any old man, like any other man who settles for less,
he doesn't give a damn about where he's going, what happens next.
Where he might be tomorrow, or the next day, or the rest.

Pebbles

At night, Mother murmurs with another voice
in the dim lamplight of the living room.
The eavesdropper sits like crumpled paper,

a first draft peering through the banisters above,
small fingers tapping, white knuckled, dinosaur pyjamaed,
scruffy eyed. Teaspoons clink awake in mugs,

monotone voices sink into drowsiness. The dog yaps
at silence, ears sharp against the world, unwelcome
and strange in its shadow. She pulls against her chain,

argues with the dark, scribbles out clouds that never
answer back. Lights plink out in the upstairs windows
like pebbles thrown into a well, swallowed out of sight.

In the belly of darkness, secrets are whispered and stick
to the spider web empty rooms. Words are left
hanging. They fall, but never land.

Why Mum Bit Her Tongue at the Crematorium

My mum had a blister on the base of her thumb,
a tiny pocket of skin like a piece of white rice.
She held peeled satsumas and broke them like eggs.
She always had an orange lining under her fingernails,
a moss that creeps into the gaps between bricks. She sliced
an apple in half with a pocket knife as she held it in her palm,
popped one sliver in her mouth, then gave the rest to me.
When the flesh turned brown I didn't want to eat it.
The apple wedges were decaying teeth in her wrinkled hand.
She told me they were exactly the same as they had been
before, just older now. The apple didn't taste any different.
If anything, it was tougher – flesh like polystyrene.

She burnt the back of her hand on the oven grate –
the skin was puckered into a swollen pair of lips,
the flesh around it bruised black. She burnt it
so often she didn't even notice now – the marks
of old brandings still lingered on her knuckles.
She was with her mother at the end. She tells me
the good parts – playing bingo in the living room
of the care home, the buzz of a full house. She doesn't
tell me about the hand holding, liver spotted
and wrinkled like onion skin, wiping the yellow boil
of mashed potato off the corner of her lip,
reminding her where those white lilies came from.

Baba's Burgers

She cups the chicken fat of her belly under her blue uniform
before stretching it down, pins back the tanned bread roll
of her earlobe with spat out gum so she can hear everything.

Then she reaches up to straighten a shelf of Coco Pops,
smiles as he walks past down the aisle brushing a hand
across her arse. She doesn't turn – she knows who it is.

Later she'll stand outside, bleach blonde and peach skin
doused in sticky vanilla, a red pimple like a fire ant on her cheek,
heels wobbling under the swell of her ankles. By ten,

they'll be huddled over the counter in Baba's Burgers, giggling
as Baba flips her brown discs of meat like beetles on their backs.
They'll watch wet-mouthed as white grease spits out like foam.

Right then, she'll be lightyears away from 7am, stacking tinned tuna,
wearing a name badge reading *Fait* because the *h* has peeled off.
The night is hungry, its tongue drools into the open doorway.

What I Know About Alice

She is 23 and has a rattlesnake for a tongue.
She is mentholated plutonium, chewing gum.
Man, you can breathe her in, glow from the inside out.
She told me her father used to get giddy on petrol fumes
and caterpillar dance down the street.

I saw her hold an orange between her teeth
and unpeel it with her tongue (her party trick).
She hates it when the lights in public toilets flicker
but don't go out. *I mean, at least commit to something!*
she once shouted, imagining them as glass eggs

for the flies buzzing to get out. Then she's curled up
in a cubicle with her head in the toilet at 3am,
pushing out the old year through her oesophagus
like a woman in labour, cleaning out the insides
her mother gave her. You know what else?

When Alice was 10 she wanted to be a model.
Before that she just wanted to be funny.
Now she just wants enough money to sooth
the tumour-like ache growing hair and teeth
and a conscience deep in the pit of her.

There was a time when Alice thought
that babies just rolled off tongues like compliments.
Then she learnt they tapeworm rip through your gut.
Now she knows you're stuck with what you get,
like a single bedroom catacomb, like a headache

that splits her ears into eggshells, like a body
slowly turning into an apology letter to itself.
At night, she holds the moon and rocks it
in warm arms, sharpening its milk teeth,
saying *there, there. There, there.*

Candyfloss

You bought a plastic tub of candyfloss from the supermarket
and ate it in front of me. Your teeth turned into pink fairy lights,
little orange-pith strings in between them. You dug
your fingers into fluffed cotton, got it stuck under your nails –
let it dissolve on your tongue like a lump of butter
on a hot frying pan. You pulled off a hairball clump
and gave it to me, sticky playdough moulded by your fingertips.

Under the streetlight outside Sainsbury's cars skidded through puddles –
your teeth were rusted round the edges with pink sugar.
That was the same night you swatted a fly and killed it, blackberry
body squashed against your bare arm. You brushed it off and wiped
your hand on your skirt, but I still let you take me here. I let you
tell me all about Mars. I let you tell me about a dream you had
where you broke out of jail and I was there but I wasn't important.

Last night you had a breakdown and cut your hair and now it bobs
around your ears like the blonde cap of a mushroom. You run your fingers
through it and act surprised when they touch empty air. I like it this way.
The skin around your nose piercing was a raw pimple, a small insect
on your face. When I chewed the candyfloss it had the texture of dry grass.
You cat-licked the pink stickiness off your palm; told me it tasted
salty. It didn't, but I still said you were right. You like it when you're right.

Poltergeist

It hovers by the microwave at night, bent forward
with its not-hands on its not-knees so it can watch a bowl
of chilli eternally spinning. The light inside the box hums,
and it waits for the pop of kidney beans like seed pods,
the pepper skin wrinkling like a burnt tongue.

It can put its not-head through the glass door if it wants,
feel the electricity dart through its thumb-print of a brain,
but it doesn't. It knows not to interrupt before the countdown
ends. It pretends to help out, wafts a not-hand over
the crumb-covered table, never brushing anything into a pile.

I put a plate out for it now, to stop it from lurking
while I eat. It sits there like a lonely thought, feeding
off the warmth radiating from the meat. There are gaps
in the air where I think it is trying to make conversation, so I listen
to it not-talk, make sure to laugh at its not-jokes,

its stirring a not-finger around the sauce. After, it lingers
with its not-hands in washing up water, moves them
through plates pancake stacked on the draining board,
tries to remember what it was to feel the wet heat
between fingers, to cast a shadow on the tiles.

Dumplings

My roommate is teaching me to make dumplings.
I slide my knife through lemons that split
apart like burnt rocks. The pips bubble and spit
as if they're simmering. He says he likes the smell.
It reminds him of his grandma, whose hands
rolled bread dough between dusky palms,
crusting flour into cracked skin.

She kneaded kernels of pepper into warm pastry
with bloodied fingers, like tarmac being pressed
into soft palms. Baking powder stuck under her
fingernails, knuckles peeling like ripe plums.
He liked to add salt to his. Real sea salt crumbled into
glass that he rubbed into the wound of the dough.

His grandma lost her three front teeth
to a bony fist. She talked with a lisp,
shot saliva when she spoke, became unable
to say her grandson's name. He used to pull
the thin hangnails off his fingers
until the skin around them was raw meat.

She would squeeze lemon juice into the cuts
and hold his wrists when he squirmed. She pushed
the pips out and they landed on his fingernails
like pale insects. She said when you leave yourself vulnerable
you must expect pain. There's something about pain that smells sour.
Sounds like the crunch of bones around a soft-skinned fruit.

Dates are the toughest. Their skin is old leather, you have to stretch
them with your teeth until they snap like rubber. He teaches me
a trick his grandma taught him, soaking them in warm water
to tender the skin. I don't like dates. I find them too bitter and veiny
but my roommate insists on folding them in with raw fingers,
telling me I'll learn to like them, over time.